# How to Haiku?

Kaushal Suvarna

Copyright © 2023 Kaushal Suvarna



Made with ❤ on the Notion Press Platform

www.notionpress.com

To those who want to learn haiku
– and those who think they know

No verse is free for the man who wants
to do a good job.
There is only good verse, bad verse, and
chaos.


– T S Eliot
Father of the free verse

# ACKNOWLEDGEMENTS


## To Nilesh,

without our constant discussions, indeed quarrels over art,
cinema, music, and life in general, I would never have taken
haiku seriously or understood the visual aspects of it.

## To William Erickson,

my own voice echoing across the other side of the globe,
in more natural, softer tones;
for keeping poetry alive and kicking, even in this world.

## To Nimish,

for pushing me to look even closer.

## To Sheryl,

for all the humour.

## To Abhishek,

for your heartfelt review of Siamese Compassion,
you truly got me brother.
And for getting me to write that article about haiku.

## To Manjusha,

for the first review of Siamese Compassion from a total
stranger, and for being strangers no more.

## To Chandana,

the Queen of Haiku Jam, my almost-friend,
for agreeing there was something wrong with the way
people write haiku, and for believing that I had a key.

## To smartphones and macro lenses

To Sonali,
with a finger in every poetic pie in the city,
I would not have met as many confused poets without you!
But seriously, for all your love, appreciation, and promotion.


To Maha Mata Mahrukh,
your recommending Siamese Compassion to so many of your
friends gave me a desire to publish again;
and for your smoked Baingan Bhartaas!


To Anjali,
for your innocence.


To Vyoma,
for always being there, for your love of the sea,
for being you.


To Jaspriya,
for all the fun, support, strength, and for dropping by,
even if only occasionally. And for the *Chinaars!*


To Achita,
even in your absence, for reminding us all, of the fragrance
and textures that only you bring to poetry.


To Shamik,
still waiting for you by the window sills.


To Manjoo,
for your desire to learn, despite everything.


To Bindu,
your crazy lines, your warm greetings.

To Durgesh,
for your feverish, yet systematic, pursuit of passion,
your love of nature, pictures, language, and poetry.

To Vinay,
for being the one, all these years, with whom
I can have fun in English.

To Sagun,
for being my promoter, much more than my shy self.

To Kashyap,
for being an ocean of calm, all these years.

To Anshul,
for the fun and friendship, without questions.

To Prajakta,
all the ups, all the downs, all the love, all these years.

To Pappa,
for all the trouble, and yet,
for being the decent man you were.

To Mummy,
there is no one kinder, no one stronger.

To Irina Guliaeva,
for your madness; for knowing, even today,
that haiku is much more than form and nature.

To Ivan Akhmatov,
your poetry makes this world better.

# How to Haiku?

A haiku guidebook for the practically confused soul

Kaushal Suvarna

# Horseradish!

# Meat n potatoes

# Digestif

# Further reading

# How to Haiku?

A haiku guidebook for the practically confused soul

# Horseradish!

I like you
little flower
without a name

# What is this book about?

What even is haiku?

No seriously, before I go about teaching you, the reader, how to write haiku, do we even have an agreement as to what it is that we are trying to learn?

Turns out there is no consensus in the literary world.

What!
You may yell, of course we know what haiku is; it is a Japanese short poem, written in 3 lines, in 17 syllables, 5-7-5, everyone knows that!

You write about nature. You use seasonal words, what were they called again, *Kigo* yes.
You use a *cutting word*, whatever that means, and whatever it's called (psst, it's called a *Kireji*).

And you rhyme.
Or wait, do you rhyme?

And while you have a question, it is good to have questions they say, do you always write about nature?

Do you need to write in 3 lines? What about those modern hipsters who write *Monoku* – do they really write in one line, or even just one word?!

And then do I really need to count all the way up to 17?

Also, should I learn Japanese?

# To count or…

First things first, I don't know Japanese – this is an English book and we are writing haiku in English.

That out of the way, what about this whole syllable-counting business? Well, read this:

> (5) *ka-re e-da ni*
> (9!) *ka-ra-su no to-ma-ri-ke-ri*
> (5) *a-ki no ku-re*

That's Japanese, which of course you and I do not understand, so here's a translation:

> on a withered branch
> a crow is perched
> late Autumn eve
> **- Bashō**

Now note who wrote that, the poet's name is written in a bigger font below the translated haiku above (and if you do not know who **Bashō** is, why are you even reading this book).

And now count the number of syllables in each line of the original Japanese text (for the morbidly lethargic among you, I have already given the counts to the left of each line).

And for good measure, now even add them up; are there 17 syllables in a 5–7–5 format?

No? Good!

So, if it works for Bashō, who are us mere mortals to disagree; we are not going to count!

## *On* a *more* serious note,

even if one did want to count, Japanese syllables, called *On* or *Morae* in haiku, are generally much shorter than their English counterparts, because the vowels are much more frequent, and shorter too.

Nearly every syllable in Japanese haiku is a consonant + vowel pair; consider the beautiful and perfectly haiku-ready Japanese word for the Cuckoo – *Hototogisu,* exactly 5 syllables.

On the other hand, consider a word like *strengths* in English. Yes, that's just one syllable!

Of course, that was extreme (to make a point) but even if you wanted a very strict version of the Japanese haiku form in English, the length would be closer to 11–13 English syllables, not 17.

Besides, this whole idea of counting syllables is *moronic* (pardon the pun), no one actually, seriously writes like that!

Furthermore, in poetry, as also in haiku, syllables (or *on* or *morae*) are not a length counter – they are a *time-keeping* device, much like rhythm in music, or dance, but more on that later (or check out the chapter *Rhythm and Blues*, if you absolutely can't wait).

## But at least 3 lines?

Ok, read this:

> bountiful harvests
> in the Sun's land, none
> **- Iio Sōgi**

Now I can forgive you for not knowing **Sōgi**, he is not as famous (I've even written his name in a smaller font below the haiku), and after all he wrote this somewhere in the 1400s, only about 200 years before Bashō.

But wait, you say; that could be 2 lines in the English translation, but 3 in the original Japanese!

Ha-ha! Clever, aren't we, almost got me there:

> *sumeba nodokeki*
> *hi no moto mo nashi*

Bonus points if you counted that's not 17 syllables. Not 17 Japanese syllables, I mean.

# Then what to do?

Fret not, we will go into all these, and even more questions, and options, one by one. Read on, all will be clear in a few chapters.

For starters, you can write haiku in 2 or 3 lines.

Modern haiku can also be written in a single line, in which case, it is called a *Monoku* and is often shorter.

However, if we wish to write as close to the classical form as possible, I would recommend 2-3 lines, and about 11-13 English syllables.
And as we are not going to count syllables, that comes to roughly 5-9 English words.

But 5-9 is still quite indefinite; exactly how long, you ask?

It is traditionally said that a haiku be only long enough to speak in one breath. I find this to be the perfect example, so try to base the length of your work on this:

> *furuike ya*
> *kawazu tobikomu*
> *mizu no oto*

If you didn't already know, that's the Japanese text to perhaps the most famous haiku in the world:

> this old pond
> a frog jumps in
> – the sound of water
> **- Bashō**

That's my translation and yes, there is a difference between saying *the sound of water* and saying *splash!* as it is often translated. But I'll leave it as home exercise for you to understand that for yourselves.

Coming back to the length, note this is just my recommendation if you plan to write classically, and you may choose to write longer or shorter, and indeed everyone does, depending on what is being said, and how. However, I've seen people write very long lines or even entire essays – please don't.

So, summing up, that's 5-9 regular English words, of any size – long words, short words or even prepositions and articles like *a*.

Speaking of articles, yes, it is customary to drop articles where relevant and convenient and, just like poetry, other grammatical license can be taken.

Also, often plural is eschewed so e.g., in haiku, *crow* may mean a particular crow or a flock or even the entire *crow-kind*, depending on the context (or interpretation).

And BTW, we generally don't rhyme (even in poetry).

# 'tis the season to write *Hokku*

Yes, you read that right, the word *Haiku* was coined much later (somewhere toward the end of the 19th century) by **Masaoka Shiki**.
It was earlier known as *Hokku*, and if you wish to write *Hokku*, even today, you need to have a proper *season word*, traditionally known as *Kigo*, e.g., *Plum blossoms* for Spring, or say, for Monsoon a *frog* or a *toad* etc.

However, for lesser mortals like us, merely writing *Haiku*, not *Hokku*, often with barely 5 or 6 regular English words, a simple seasonal reference will do, say *Winter morn*, or *Spring walk* or other such banalities.

But of course, we don't just write about seasons, we can also write about other natural phenomena and objects say the *sea*, or *rainbows* in the *sky* or *moonlight*, or the *Milky Way*, or *full moons* or *crescent moons*, and such references, being natural enough, are okay for us.

Then there is the modern charge, folks who say that we exist in much more than *nature* now, and we can talk of *buildings*, and *trains* and *machinery*, what have you.

For them *Kigo* is not a *season word* so much as a *key word* – just a context to the set the scene of the haiku.

Keep that in mind, if not as a modern haiku poet, then at least as a reader/writer of haiku in modern times.

And finally, there are the *empaths*, like yours truly, who say that human nature is also *nature* and why not write about guilt, and delight, and hope, and jealousy – the whole gamut.

Traditionally this is not called *Haiku* but rather *Senryu*.

Here's a fun challenge though, find anyone who can always tell the distinction.

# What about the *Kireji* though?

It is also imperative for it to be called a *Hokku* for it to have a *Kireji*, loosely translated as the *cutting word*.
Well, I'll cut to it – there's no equivalent in English for the *cutting word*.
I'll give you a moment for that to sink in.

...


Ok, now I'm so done; let's all just pack our bags and go home?

Now now, hold on!
Firstly, we are writing *Haiku*, not *Hokku*, so let's not fuss – no *cutting word*, no problem!

But most important, let us try to understand what the *cutting word* even is, and see if we can't simulate something.


What the *cutting word* is, is a kind of conjunction or punctuation or exclamation that *cuts* the text of the haiku in two phrases that somehow contrast each other, or create a different meaning or interpretation when thus juxtaposed against each other.
The cutting word puts the preceding phrase in a new context or sometimes even makes the whole haiku cyclical when used at the end.

In short, it is generally the thing that creates the *aha moment* that is so highly prized in haiku (I'm sure even folks with passing interest have heard this about haiku).

We will see (later) how using the correct images and proper words will achieve this shift of focus.

And if nothing else works we, the English, have the *dash* – more on that little secret later too.


We will also mull over whether this sensationalism isn't perhaps overrated and may be piercing simplicity, not *cutting words* or stunning imagery, is the soul of haiku

# Deep shit

That conveniently brings me to the next topic.
So, we know now how to write haiku (yeah, you wish, if it were that simple, we wouldn't need the rest of this book, but fine I hear you, we can at least start writing) but what about *what to write about in haiku?*

I mean sure, you talk about nature, but is that it?
Talk about flowers and trees, or do we also talk of birds and bees (if you get my drift)?

Also, you might have heard them say that haiku can encapsulate all of Zen, and talk of hidden truths and help you achieve stillness and even enlightenment, and what not!
So naturally you may feel like you have to talk about something deep like philosophy or the oneness of humanity or at the very least about global warming.

Where do you even begin to acquire that kind of wisdom (of course who has time to read the classics) or moral fibre, short of volunteering to work for rescue efforts in Ukraine or the Great Barrier Reef (or do they have *Yoga* classes for that that you aren't in the know of)?

Well, luckily this author is your friend, so stop grabbing at reused straws, and just take a deep breath.
Trust me, you'll need it to read the haiku that follows:

*waga oya no*
*shinuru toki ni mo*
*he o kokite*

Sorry, for a while there I forgot that we don't do Japanese, so here goes nothing:

> even in the moments
> that my father lay dying
> I was merrily farting
> **- Yamazaki Sōkan**

Now despite the 90s charm (I mean 1990s) let me reassure you this was written very squarely in late 1400s-early 1500s.

And while this was widely criticised, it was not berated, as you may think, and as *The Classic Tradition of Haiku* informs us, for its *scatological* (*love of excrement*, nice word, everyone should know it) leanings but rather for disrespecting elders.

Now I'm sure you, the modern 20th/21st century (boomer or millennial or whatever they are called these days) writer, won't be held back by such old-fashioned considerations but it's always good to know shit works, and not just in this *Twitter* culture, it has worked for centuries.

You may also be pleased to know that there are haiku about loins, and other areas, and not necessarily written by perverted men but by respectable women too:

> Moonflowers —
> a woman's skin
> when you see
> **- Chiyo-ni**

and the Japanese text (since you don't trust me):

> *yūgao ya*
> *onago no hada no*
> *miyuru toki*

But c'mon you are not prudes and perhaps I judge you unfairly. But then again, some of us might not exactly be thrilled to find that there are references to homosexuality (okay, fine for some folks today) and even paedophilia (definitely not fine for most of us today) in some of these haiku, and by some very respected poets (I'm not going to name names, do your own research).

Perhaps I have cured your insistence on deep meaning and philosophy but then again, perhaps you are desensitised by *Game of Thrones*, you say that's how these things roll, and spirituality and grooming have gone hand in hand for thousands of years (if you know you know, if not, watch the film *Spotlight*).

I apologise for the dark detour, but you wanted enlightenment – well this here it is!

Life is beautiful, life sucks, the timing of things can be weird, people do horrible things, people go through horrible things, people help others (even animals and plants) expecting really nothing in return; and flowers and sunsets and moonlight and summer rains do soothe tired bodies and mend broken hearts all of a sudden, for no tangible reasons either...
The word *Zen* not only means attention, etymologically it is just a sound change of the word *Dhyana*, it literally *is* attention!

So, all philosophical bullshit aside, that is what haiku, at its finest, hopes – to pay attention!

Attention to these little things that happen, and how they affect us, internally, and everything at large. And to show, to someone who hasn't paid attention, that both are the same – the world within, and the world without!

And that grief, pleasure, life, death, misery, humour, coping, growth, nature, reflection, it's all one movement in harmony – the same shit!

And thus, perhaps you, the would-be haiku poet, will also see that *Zen*, *enlightenment*, *oneness* are just words – glorified and romanticised hand–me–downs that we have been trying to get in touch with, with no idea where to even begin or what it even means to reach there!
And, if at all one does, how would you know, how does it feel?

Is it even a real state or just a story to brush all this ugliness under the carpet and make ourselves feel better, even if for a while?
Pay attention, that is all haiku asks, and that is all that *Zen* is.

Pious, evil, afraid, hypocritical, whatever we humans are, this consciousness that we have, perhaps we are the only beings on this planet capable of looking at this apathetic world, making interpretations and finding some semblance of meaning and lending some iota of beauty to this chaos!

We are the Universe reflecting on itself, as they say…

And while this may be a great responsibility that perhaps you are now in no mood to carry, given my blaspheming of your whole idea of *enlightenment*, or perhaps you are now just too disillusioned by all this darkness, let us remember to call each thing by its proper name, and note that the word *Haiku* splits as

> *Hai - play*
> *Ku - verse*

And this is what it is all about!
You can talk of deep things, you can talk of great hurts, you can also talk of disillusionment or whether this world is shitty or if you just don't give a shit anymore!
Or you can talk of nothing worth any import at all, even just a plain old fart!


Or perhaps you don't agree with me, or don't even believe me, or perhaps you can always find that ray of sunshine behind every cloud and fill everything around you with rainbows – you may be that person, and well, more power to you.

What you write is not just up to you – it is you!
It is the sharing of this human experience, not clever words, that is prized in haiku.

Life is short, our joys ephemeral and sorrows transient. Despite the intensities and immediacy of our feelings, the world goes on with or without us, without any of us posers and without Bashō…

So, remember to have fun. It is *hai-ku* after all 😊
Write about anything that you like, anything at all!

And, to paraphrase Oscar Wilde, since the only thing worse than being a poser is looking like a poser, write about something that you actually know – your favourite flowers, your cat, the beach, your irritating boss, your immediate surroundings, moonlight, gutters...

Haiku is about your reflections in the moment, so let them be your moments.
And we will love to read about them (if you share them well).

# Haiku is NOT poetry! - Final thoughts (we start soon, I promise)

So, before I let you all loose, one last knot to tie and thing to remember – this will please the lay folks among us who have never written any poetry or found it hard and, no doubt, piss the poets off who are, no doubt, now staring at me intensely.

While haiku can be written poetically and while the thoughts and images presented may be poetic, or even meaningful, haiku is largely a visual medium – though delivered through words.
Read that again!

Poets have a tendency to keep on talking, even though good art always asks to *show, not tell* (yeah, you have heard that warning before).

Clever words and phrases can always be used to direct attention or make a point, but at the heart of haiku is the ability to present clear images.
If you doubt that, know that haiku is taught in the most esteemed film schools across the world.

Much of the artistry in haiku lies in *framing*, as it were, your thought on the *screen* of the reader's mind.

And then, frame by frame, image by image, shifting the perspective of the reader from one idea to another – there's your *aha moment*, that everyone dies for!

In haiku, as in *cinema*, the poetry happens in the reader's mind.

This requires a different way of thinking, and of seeing the world, compared to how we generally do poetry; and this can be very intimidating and frustrating in the beginning, especially for poets.

Take your time, be patient, and the exercises that follow will guide us slowly but surely to achieve this *mode switch* – and that certainly is what it is, let no one have any illusions, it's an entirely different approach of looking at things…

Welcome to haiku, let's play!

# Meat n potatoes

the lilies
bruised pink –
hard rains

# Ex. #0.5 Set up a natural scene

One of the core skills in haiku, even more than the ability to speak in images, is to be able to get to the essence of things; and so, in Exercise 1 we will learn to talk about a thing using one of its visual (or other) characteristics.

But remember we only have 5 to 9 words to convey what is in our heart. That is a prohibitively short space, and that is a problem for both of our two sets of readers viz.
- poets, who can't say anything in short at all, and
- non-poets, who perhaps fear to write even 5 words

So before getting down and dirty, we will try a pre-exercise, just to get used to the idea of putting your thoughts concisely.
Now we could write about anything, since this is just to get you used to writing very short verses, however since we aim to write classical haiku (whenever possible) let's try to set up a natural scene.

You can choose anything you like, beaches, the moon, your pets at home, dogs in the park, whatever you generally see around and are familiar with. It doesn't need to have any depth or even artistic merit.

The goal is to just write about some natural event or phenomenon that you have witnessed or some natural thing that you like, say some bird or flower, in about 5 to 9 words.

So, try that, write a few pieces by yourself, and then read further.

# Example – how to ~~write~~ read a haiku

Okay, hopefully you were able to write a few, and have got the blood flowing, both in your fingers and your brain.

Let us now look at a simple setup by the Master, Bashō himself (it has more than 9 words but it's a translation so let that go for now, and still not bad for just 11 words, and you'll know if you tried writing):

> on a withered branch
> a crow is perched
> late Autumn eve
> **- Bashō**

We have seen this in the previous section, but it is worth studying deeper; this happens to be Bashō's other most revered haiku, second only to the frog one.

Why?
He apparently doesn't even seem to be talking about anything here, nothing deep at all for sure!

Let us see, what is he doing? Firstly, what is this about? How does one even go about reading (into) this?
Questions, questions...

Well, let's try to take a systematic approach, let's ask the basic questions; what is the most essential thing for it to be a haiku (*hokku*, in Bashō's time)? The seasonality, of course.

So, Bashō is talking about *an Autumn evening, late Autumn evening*, by some translations. Now that can be read as *late in the evening*, so almost night some time in Autumn, or it can be read as *late in Autumn*, so almost Winter.

And what happens on this *dark* Autumn evening?
A *crow* comes, another dark creature.

Notice that one must read this visually, the mood is being set, and it's easy to see if you pay attention.

But in addition to the visual cues, the crow is traditionally considered an omen of dark things, so Bashō is speaking symbolically as well.

He could have referenced any *Winter* bird, say a *Crane*, he chose *Crow* for a reason; as a reader we need to see these subtle choices, and as a wannabe haiku writer we need to ask these questions of ourselves when putting any word on paper – we often only have 5 or 6 of them, so we better weigh each word as if it were gold.


And what happens with the crow, then?
It doesn't just fly around on that fading Autumn evening; it doesn't just come and sit on the top branch or *somewhere* on the tree.
No, the crow comes and sits *on a withered branch*.

Notice the purposefulness of the imagery.
See how subtly Bashō piles up motif upon motif of darkness, withering, fading, dying, things coming to an end, and builds up a melancholic mood.

And all that without saying a word directly about his grief or fears; perhaps he was pondering his own death, or the passing of a loved one…

Or perhaps just the setting sun, the advent of Winter made him sad, only for a moment. It is not for us to know.


A poet would have let us know!
A poet would have drowned us with gilded platitudes of his immense grief, told us exactly how badly it affects him and tried everything to tug at our heart strings.

But haiku is not about talking like that, so Bashō just shows us a dreary scene of one Autumn evening, when a weary crow came to rest on a withering tree (branch).

Still, a sensitive reader is pushed in the right direction, cleverly nudged by the writer, and feels the desolate mood of the evening, perhaps himself being world-weary; the well-placed hints of things coming to an end bringing out the reader's own insecurities and suddenly hitting him/her in the core.


And thus, one man's reflections in the moment are seamlessly, even wordlessly, transferred to another!
The reader, most probably, is not sad about the same things that Bashō was. But suffering, being universal, one man's pondering on his existence reaches another, even across the ages!

The content of individual grief is not important, what matters is that they both grieve.
We all do…


And that, kids, is how it is done.

# Ex. #0.5 More examples

So, remember when I told you that this exercise of *setting up a natural scene* didn't really matter, that it was just a pre-exercise to get you used to writing very short verses…
Yeah, well I lied.

If you read that analysis of Bashō above, it must be immediately clear to you how powerful it can be just to set up a scene well. Everything can be conveyed just through a carefully selected and well-written scene.

All the exercises that follow, and there are many, are mostly techniques, ways to doll up your scene. But if your setup itself is weak then, as they say, you can put lipstick on a pig.

If you take nothing else from me, even if you stop reading the book from here on ahead, just write a good *natural* scene and, most of the time, that should be a good haiku – a moment conveyed with honesty will ring true with the reader.


Just remember, it's not a documentary – don't be clinical or robotic; we are trying to convey *what we suddenly felt in a given moment, looking at something in nature.*
On the other hand, by convey, I mean *show* that, don't write an autobiography or an *emo* pop song.

If you are getting mixed signals, it's because it's a fine line that is different for everyone, and all this is easier said than done; so, a few more examples to get us started.

- Anjali, @AnjaliPatwardhan29

While not at the same level as Bashō (and that's the point, of course, not everything has to be) note how **Anjali** simply evokes the mood of heavy rains in the incessant monsoon and the nostalgia of childhood with commonplace observation – kids play with paper boats and leaves flow down tiny rivulets.

Perhaps when she saw the rains and had this thought, kids were not actually sailing paper boats (do kids even do that these days?); perhaps just the drifting leaves reminded her of that, but she makes that connection and we are transported back to our childhood.

Beautifully done and in only 6 words.

Also note the simplicity of her words; while I said earlier that we need to choose the correct words, to weigh each word as if it were gold, we must remember that all that glitters is not gold.
Sure, you need to have a good vocabulary to find the right words, but to just use big or flashy words for the heck of it is like going to the gym to build a good body and then staring at yourself in the mirror...

Remember no one likes a wise-ass no matter how great that ass looks in yoga pants.

Simplicity is key, especially when you intend to convey things so deep and touching to the reader, emotions so universal and yet so personal. You want to quietly enter the reader's heart, not clobber them over the head and daze them into submission.

On that note, read this:

> shadows grew longer
> under the autumn *Chinaars*
> I lay still
> - **Jaspriya, @JaspriyaGandhok, @life_in_post_its**

This is slightly longer than my preferred length, but how wonderfully written – one can almost feel the stillness of a lazy, shady afternoon!
And the stunning visual of the orange-red starry Maple-like leaves – one almost feels transported to a movie!

But also note how **Jaspriya** cleverly contrasts that stillness with the slow passage of time anyway, with the phrase *shadows grew longer.* And so, despite the picturesque setting one might even feel a bit melancholy over the steady yet firm grip of time over our little pleasures…
Such passage of time and such subtle contradictions are both highly prized in haiku, and this is done so beautifully and so visually here!

Another thing is the pacing of the words, along with the slightly longer text, makes it go a bit slowly in your mind, as you read.

That's a simple yet educative example of how good poets use rhythm subtly to create certain effects and lull, or arouse, certain feelings. In this case, it goes perfectly with the author lazing around till the evening.

Note that, as mentioned previously, syllables are not for counting, but to manipulate rhythm; one should know when to use the long ones, the short ones, the hard ones, the soft ones.

That is one of the most essential things to poetry, but since most poets directly jump into *free verse*, without formal training (yes one needs to train to be a poet, just as a musician or a dancer, to develop this sense of rhythm), this is lost, unless one has a good *ear*.

Natural spoken language does have a rhythm, so conversational poems often work, especially in this current trend of *spoken-word poetry* with dramatic recitation, and there is a place for that.

However, in written poetry, that's meant to be read in silence, and especially in a short form like haiku, every consonant stressed and every half-beat skipped can have an impact, for better or worse. We will formally learn a bit more about rhythm later, but in the meantime pay attention to that.

Now, one last example to summarise this lesson; set up is so vital:

> grey clouds
> moving away
> sills still wet
> **- Shamik Sen**

Of course, this can be read as a simple depiction of rains passing by your locality. But if you pay attention to the sudden shift in rhythm of the 3rd line, you may notice the hint of grief cleverly tucked in there by the author.

That, along with the contrast of wetness in your home despite the rains having gone, and the use of the image of *grey clouds*, clearly suggests the author means more than he is letting on; he mourns a lost relation (or some such loss), he is coping, but still hurt...

And that, fellow poets and lay readers, is the beauty of haiku – all that can be said without saying anything at all!

Just find the right image and set up your scene with finesse. Don't goad the reader, trust their maturity to find the right way home through the terrain you've laid out...

And when they find it, aha!

# Ex. #1 Write about the characteristic/s of a thing/scene

Finally, we are here, you must be thanking your stars, no telling what weird detours this author might take!

I feel you, but fear not, the most important, tortuous, and arduous lessons are behind us, it should be smooth sailing from here on.

Having said that, do remember to practice what you learn, don't rush through the exercises, just reading them. Even if you think you have got a hang of everything, it is important to actually do it yourself!
I can't stress that enough, write, write a lot, and keep revising till you are happy with the technique…


That said, let's move on to our first exercise proper.
As mentioned before, this is the most important feature of haiku – we want to get to the essence of something.

We want to talk about a thing, preferably a natural object or event, by showing one (or sometimes more) of its defining characteristics.
Say you want to write something about a dog, what defines *dog-ness*?

There are no marks for guessing and there are no correct answers, you could say whatever it means to you!

So, some may say *loyalty*, some may say that a dog always *barks*, or that its tail keeps *wagging*, or its long, wet *tongue* or cold *nose* – all are valid.

However, we need something we can work with, say you had a camera to shoot a dog, it is easy to show a wagging tail or tongue; how do you show loyalty, in a frame or two?

So, to start with, let's look at a very simple example:

> the pink
> of Summer —
> Bougainvillea

Of course, there's nothing here, we are simply focusing on the *pinkness* of the *Bougainvillea* vine/tree. The flowers can, of course, be in other colours but typically the bright pink or magenta variants are common and stunning, so we use that characteristic to focus on.

However, the plant is a Summer staple, and in a way, we are using the *Bougainvillea* itself as a characteristic of *Summer!*
And we gel all that together smartly with the way its phrased – *the pink of Summer* – employing a bit of *metonymy* to add a dash of flair to the simplistic piece.

Additionally, the deep pinkness contrasts with the blinding yellow hues of the hot Indian Summer Sun, crafting an overall rosy picture, portraying the harsh Summer heat in a poetic way instead.

Obviously, visuals work great in haiku, they are also easy for the reader to get (or visualise 😆), but don't ignore the other senses as well – for example invoking the sense of smell or even touch can work wonders, though rarer in haiku coz it's harder to pull off.

Sound is fairly common in haiku though, easiest being the use of *onomatopoeia* –

> rat-tat-tat
> a gun on my head –
> the Mynah

focusing, of course, on the *Mynah* bird's default irritating sound (it is a great impostor though, and can be sweet if it chooses).

Note also the visual, the headache caused by the sharp noise compared to a gunshot to the head!

You can also use *alliteration* and other devices to create sound and link it to the object you are talking about, so the reader is mentally reminded of it.

This is not the easiest to pull off in English if we are aiming for the classical length or fewer words, but here's a lovely example in Japanese (also highlighting the wonderful exploitation of the short syllables in the language):

> *kokoro koko ni*
> *naki ka nakanu ka*
> *hototogisu*

Can you guess by the alliteration, what it is about?
If you thought *crow*, that would have been close, but there was a hint in the last line, if you have paid attention in the earlier chapters.

*Hototogisu,* of course, being a *Cuckoo:*

is my heart not in
or has it not sung
– the Cuckoo
- **Ihara Saikaku**

35

This brings us to an important discussion in haiku, that I don't see anyone discussing at all – see how much is lost in the translation (that's just part A of this discussion).

# An important discussion, Side A

**Saikaku's** piece, in the original Japanese text, is an exemplar of sound design in haiku. In the English translation there is not a trace of it!

If you had read only the English text, and if that text was not particularly deep or beautiful or effective, you might have wondered what was so amazing about Saikaku.

This is something you, the reader, needs to be painfully aware of when reading translations of the original Masters (or indeed of good modern Japanese or Russian haiku – yes, there is a huge haiku following in Russian, Spanish, and closer home, even in regional languages like Malayalam, Tamil).

And of course, there can be worse translations and we might be missing so much subtext of so many other pieces, or reading too much in others, things that the writers never intended.

If you are really young, and/or really free and/or really motivated, I would definitely recommend learning not just Japanese but also more about the culture and times of these writers, to gain deeper understanding of what they truly meant.

And I hope someday one of you writes more about this. In the meantime, you must make do with me 😊

# An important discussion, Side B

And that brings us to part B of this discussion – to most of us, the English translated text is all we have to understand what classical haiku is…
And despite that we have loved it!

This is a very important, and hardly-thought-about point, so let that sink in.
…


Taking the above example again, even if we knew nothing about Saikaku's sound, and we may still not know much about the hidden Japanese contexts in that piece, in particular the *cutting word*, there is no denying that it is a beautifully written piece, and that we have liked it.
What does that mean to us, as a haiku poet in the English language?

Well first, despite my recommendation above, don't bother with Japanese if you don't have the time or inclination!
Don't have regrets, there are often things we will never know of olden times and of the poet's mind, that's a fact of life, we live with it.

Besides, this book is not about reading haiku (though that's of course a big part of it) but rather on how we can write better and as accurately as possible in the conventions of the classical art, given the constraints of our knowledge, and our language – do remember even if we knew everything, we still don't have the short syllables or the *cutting words*.

Second, as mentioned previously, sounds, figures of speech, *cutting words* to shift focus, all these are techniques, to enhance the base haiku – if that itself is not great, or at least decent, why even bother?

At best we are indulging in a display of vocabulary or exercises in *form*, and sadly that's what it is in much of professional haiku or poetry or even cinema or so-called modern art – a glorified husk of graceful kitsch, a charming shell without soul!

So, looking again at this English text:

> is my heart not in
> or has it not sung
> – the Cuckoo
> **- Ihara Saikaku**

we can still decipher some techniques; one, that the writer deflects from himself to the Cuckoo, and he keeps the suspense till the end. Also, the way the rhythm falters, rises, and then breaks, that too helps with the uneasiness of the piece, mirroring the writer's uneasy mind.

And so, despite the writer not being entirely upfront with us, one can realise the upheavals of his buzzing mind; clearly, he is disturbed about something, to not have noticed the sweet sound of the Cuckoo, even though he yearns for it! He tells us, then hides, but still tells us in a roundabout way!

Of course, this is not as subtle as Bashō's crow, and this is still *more tell than show*, but not everything can be and not everyone has to be, or even wants to be, Bashō!

We are unique in our sorrows and our styles; certain traits are admired in art but we must also express the way we are!

Another silly thing that you may note is even this translation was way longer than our limit of 5 to 9 words – it was 12 (though smaller) words. So, all this is not the point of our writing at all!

A well-meant, honestly expressed piece is just as important as a well-written piece, within constraints of the art-form, of course! But, before we continue, know that these goals are often mutually incompatible!

Not every piece will be perfect; you will struggle with consistency, with spilling your heart in exactly the ways you want in the limited space you have. You may have to choose then between technical accuracy, and other creative constraints, and emotional honesty!

This too is the way of things and, as haiku poets, we take that gracefully, in our stride.

And as you will see, even in English, there is a lot of technical jugglery to do; and over the remainder of this book, we will try to learn what we mean by *well-written*...

The *well-meant* and *honestly expressed* is your responsibility!

# Ex. #1 Final example

One last example before we move on to Exercise 2; remember, we are trying to define an object by its characteristics.
And by that we typically think of *visual characteristics* like colour, shape or occasionally sound and I recommend trying to *invoke other senses* such as touch, smell, warmth, cold etc. as well.


However, as mentioned previously, the characteristic or essence of an object may sometimes be its *behaviour*, say the *wagging* of dogs, or even their *loyalty*, which we had brushed aside for the moment.

So, while that is difficult to show, it isn't impossible:

> the good fly
> dusting her feet
> outside my kitchen

Here we find the essence of a fly in its constant rubbing of its feet!
And while most of us find it yucky, and for good reason, as we don't want them anywhere near our food doing that, here the writer (yours truly, *always unless otherwise mentioned*) plays on that fear, and social distancing, and even endears the fly a little!

This is a highly cherished trait in haiku – not just the ability to notice the little things but to be able to empathise and even create a soft corner for every living, and even inanimate, being.

The roots of *Zen* and Japanese culture in general, and even *Hinduism* for that matter, are in *Animism* - and something primordial is aroused in the reader with the defending of the underdog!

Notice though, how it is done; soppy sentimentality and *romanticising* is not appreciated, and here the writer has maintained a *natural* image without personifying the fly or sweet-talking to or about it, as one is wont to do in poetry!

That is the skill, to let natural things be natural, the way they are in their place, and still find oneness, and even love, with them!

# Ex. #2 Compare or link two unrelated things with a common characteristic

Ok good folks, I hope you have practised enough, and now know to write about the essences of many natural objects, say dogs and mountains and clouds etc.
If not, do stay on exercise 1 and practise some more, because now we will up the *ante* a little; we now want to link two natural objects with one *apparently* common characteristic.

I say *apparently* because, of course, two drastically different things will not generally have the same characteristic, we are taking a bit of poetic license or being clever through words or finding a random coincidence etc.

Needless to say, let there be a creative leap between the two objects compared; don't e.g., link a *sheep* to a *goat* via *bleating*. Cast a wide net; the more disparate the objects compared, the bigger the chance to (pleasantly) surprise your reader.
And as you can imagine, this is a simple way to get that aha that you want, or at least a smile 😊

> flock of geese
> behind me
> a truck honks

I'm fairly certain everyone got that, the cry of a *goose* is also called *honking*.

While rather simple, this piece makes use of sound to connect two things, though still being quite visual. Also, if you follow the visuals, the jolt you get is sudden and more surprising, because you might be seeing a *V-shaped formation in the sky*, and suddenly the *truck behind you* shakes you out of the *reverie*, brings you down to earth, so to speak.

Note that this is intentional and mirrors the daydreaming of a person, perhaps a weary office-goer stuck in a traffic jam, in his daily grind, finding some respite in his mental escapes only to be obnoxiously pulled back to reality.

So yes, while the text itself is quite simple, and easy to read, note again, so much can be said and inferred wordlessly.

Behind the apparent simplicity, a lot of technical stuff is going on, like a duck paddling underwater (and yes, this example of the *duck* too was intentional to *callback* to the *goose* from earlier).

Strong imagery, not vocabulary – flaunt the correct mental muscles!

Another simple image:

> hot sun –
> a saltpan worker
> wipes his brow
> **- Vyoma C**

Again remember, while we are doing these exercises to define things by their characteristics, and to find commonalities, don't forget the setup! Exercise 0.5, as we had discussed at length, is the stage for all these techniques to shine on.

It is important to ground the scene, as **Vyoma** does here with the simple phrases *hot sun* and *saltpan* – that immediately drops us right into the deserted hostile environment, and naturally conjures up the image of sweating.

And then very neatly she moves the *salt* from the *pan* to the *worker's brow* – it is inevitable in its visual logic!
And thus, without any melodrama, she intimates us of the plight of these exploited labourers not just wordlessly but at a visceral level.

*Visceral, bodily* – these are words you will hear often used to describe good haiku, because it has that kind of an effect; haiku, much more than poetry, can hit you *right in the feels*.

Then again, not everything needs to be doom and gloom:

> summit to summit
> mountaineer slug

As with the final example for Exercise 1, characteristics don't need to be *physical attributes*, we can also link seemingly random things by their *behaviour.*

So here we imagine a slug (a kind of leaf-eating mollusc) chomping its way from the bottom of a branch to the top, and then moving on again to the next branch, as if it were a mountaineer on a long arduous climb 😊

Here's another *light*-hearted piece:

> a tipsy ex
> banging at the door –
> house moth

This came to me on seeing a poor moth one night banging against my bedroom door; just a fun take on its plight.

But notice the jump in thought from one compared image to the other, in especially this but also the previous example – they are so widely disconnected in reality!


And that's why haiku can make us chuckle, and cry, it's in the recognition of these little truths (though this was just an incidental joke) and finding them scattered in places one wouldn't expect!
The way we recollect happy memories and guilts totally out of place – while having a bath, sitting on the bus, looking at the stars, watching a movie, talking, or even listening, to someone else.


Something clicks, at weirdly random, even inappropriate times – *c'est la vie*.

And such is haiku.

# Ex. #3 Set up a scene and shift focus from one object to the other

This is quite like exercise 2 and in fact we have been doing it in the previous examples too, though I didn't necessarily call it to your attention.
But you may remember how in the goose example we went from staring *up* at the sky to, suddenly, the truck *behind* you.

So, in addition to just linking or even comparing things, now we will take a more cinematic approach. Think as if you were looking at the world through a camera or, better yet, binoculars.

That way you can only focus on one part of your scene, then to see the next part, or frame, perhaps you have to *pan* the camera a bit to the right, or perhaps zoom in with your binoculars on a specific person or object that needs to take *centre stage* in the scene now.

See the issue is, once you are able to write a little, you want to convey everything to the reader all at once! And then you are puzzled when the reader doesn't have the same reaction that you expected, or worse…

You show him the entire night sky and expect him to know how *Sirius* makes you happy. But how will the poor chap know where to look!

So first you show him the *Orion* constellation, you tell him it's the one that looks like a Hunter, or a *Damru*. You then *direct* him a bit leftwards, where *Canis Major* is, the one that looks like a little dog.

And then you ask him to focus on the dog's neck, and the reader realises whoa that's a bright star – the brightest in the night sky in fact and yet somehow, he had missed it – till you made the connections, for him!

That's the job of the haiku poet.
It will hit the reader, but you need to direct his attention!

The technique is different, and more visual, but the goal is the same as Exercise 1, to filter out the extraneous noise, and focus attention, both of the reader and your own, on the essential.

On that note, reminder again, before we proceed, do practice the previous exercises thoroughly; if you feel confident, now let's have a look at this:

> crescent moon
> on a park bench
> a woman smiles

Another simple piece, nothing spectacular about the image or thought per se, though it is sweet, the *crescent* of the *moon* mirroring the woman's *smile*.

However, notice how the camera moves, frame by frame, from the sky, a *wide shot*, to the bench, a *medium shot*, we are still not saying much, keeping our distance, so to speak, from the subject.

And then, when we go into a *close-up* in the 3rd line, it's as if the woman smiled when her lover finally arrived, by her bench, ending her wait!
The *camera*, actually our haiku technique, following the emotion in synch, telling her story only an image at a

time, slowly building suspense through the closing in. And perhaps, when the woman smiles, it also releases the reader's tension, built up through the slow framing technique – who knows what was to happen in the park that night!

The woman smiles, and we smile with her; and the crescent moon, the woman, and the reader all become one for a moment!


*An aside*, I recently showed this example to some schoolkids at a workshop, and they came up with a beautiful variation:

> crescent moon
> on a **rocking chair**
> a woman smiles

their idea being to add *another crescent, the base of the chair*, to the scene!

However, notice how it does much more than that; while in the park you imagine a young, or middle-aged, woman waiting for, or thinking of, her lover perhaps, the *rocking chair* immediately takes us in the mind of an older woman, reminiscing!

And which is why I said earlier that every word is worth its weight in gold, especially in English, where you have barely 5-6 words most of the time; but each image can speak so much!

Also, don't underestimate kids, they have very fertile minds!

Coming to the next example:

> Antarctic blizzard
> an Emperor stands
> egg in toes

What an epic! If I may say so myself!

Well, I can, the original scene is not mine, it's based on real life, from the outstanding nature documentary, *March of the Penguins*. O how these creatures survive these unbearable conditions!
*Emperor Penguins* protect their babies, and eggs, by holding them between their toes, their backs against crazy Antarctic *blizzards*, that sometimes go on for weeks!

Now while the content itself is outstanding, and while we are not actually comparing anything here, notice we do the same framing trick again in this haiku, but this time our *opening frame* is even grander – try to visualise this as the first scene of a movie – it immediately sets the stakes so high!

Again, though we hold back the secret of the *penguins*, the 2nd line is also so grand – *an Emperor*, the writer sets up an epic battle or expedition scene; you may perhaps be thinking *Game of Thrones* or *Ridley Scott* scale battles in the snow 😃

But then the 3rd line comes along, and it is at once a betrayal – you have been misled, there are no glorious battles here – and simultaneously a revelation, the battle was even grander than you expected!
And with an even more lovable hero – an underdog Emperor!

And notice the impact of the *close-up* on the *penguin's toes*; what a picture of parenthood!
What an image to leave the reader on!

One can't think up such stuff, truth as they say, is stranger than fiction. Well, I say, it's definitely more powerful!
Having said that, it's our job to *frame* it for maximum impact!

Also notice that while we aren't using *cutting words*, the little suspenses and betrayals in our framing do surprise the reader occasionally, and can generate that *aha moment*, or at least make them smile.

Again, note that most of our examples have been quite plain, not overdoing on either flowery language or sentimentality, or even this hankering after depth of philosophical thought; instead, mostly focusing on the purity of our observed image.

We have been so programmed about wanting to have meaning in our poetry, and especially haiku, that oftentimes poets come across as *pretentious* or *wannabes*.

And the irony is, as I hope you have felt in the pieces we have discussed so far, deep emotions and subtle truths don't need our beautification or shouting from poetic ivory towers to reach the layman!

They only need to be felt truly ourselves and then offered to the reader with clarity, in the proper light, putting the reader in the proper *frame* of mind to actually *see* them.

And on that note, one last example to cap off this exercise of *shifting focus*, this one in a more succinct, modern style:

> balloons –
> the seller's eyebags

I will not spoil this by trying to explain it, I trust your intelligence, and our discussions thus far.

Perhaps, as exercise, you can try to understand technically why this works despite its shorter length, how the setup is handled differently here, or how the comparison is itself the payoff, with no summarising 3rd line needed.

Also notice how the camera moved differently here compared to the slow zooming in of previous examples, and how the emotional effect differs due to that abrupt visual change.

BTW, remember in the chapter on *Kireji* I had mentioned that we, the English, have the *dash* – now that's a good example of its effect.

# Ex. #3.5 Big/small, near/far, here/there

This is a very important haiku lesson; this skill is highly cherished and considered one of the quintessential haiku effects. However, if you have followed along so far and practised your exercises, you will find it is just an extension of Exercise 3 i.e., shifting focus.

We have seen how to shift focus from one object, or one part of a scene, to another; we will now look at special cases where e.g.,

- one object might be near us and the other quite far, so we *shift the focus in space*; or

- one object or situation might be happening here, in the present, and may remind us of the past or take us someplace else, so we are *shifting focus in time*, or both time and space; and finally

- one object might be tiny and the other object, or the overall picture, quite big, so we are *shifting the scale* of our perspective.

Let us see some examples but before that, if you haven't, please practise the previous exercises, a lot! Also, no matter what the current exercise, don't forget Exercise 0.5 – the setup is always critical, without it there is no context to the reader as to what you are talking about or hinting to.

> tiny ant
> on collision course –
> I lift my toe

The point, and fun, of this kind of writing is not really comparing a big object to a small one, but rather to show the difference in scale and for ourselves, as well as the reader, to look at the world in a different light, almost through a child's eyes!

For the *ant*, going about its business *my toe* is a major roadblock; for me, lifting it is not even an inconvenience! The goal, as always in haiku, is achieving empathy with the other, especially animals and the helpless.

Talking about this haiku in particular, there is also a bit of fun in the imagery – the way it is written, almost as if a child were playing with a toy train, or about to bang two *Hot Wheels* cars against each other, and then changed its mind.
Such *naiveté* and innocence are prized in haiku.

On a more philosophical note, it also subtly comments that perhaps we are also as insignificant in God's plans. So, though written in a funny tone, important things can still be said, and interpreted – hallmarks of the best haiku; though we may be reaching a bit here, as all that is not obviously hinted, just that it leaves the door open to readers to go off on their own tangents.


Speaking of tangents:

> dirty red football
> kicked off the ground –
> Mars orbiting
> **- Achita Khare, @Achita_Khare**

Another beautiful shift of scale – the visual almost reminiscent of the bone scene in *Stanley Kubrick's 2001:*

*A Space Odyssey* – and simultaneously also a bit of *near/far!*

Of course, the *football* isn't actually kicked to *Mars*, but the thrill that image provides makes the wording clever nonetheless.

Also notice the little details, any odd football would have worked but **Achita** takes the time, and precious word-space, to mention that it's a *dirty red* football, not only adding direct visual reference to the redness of *Mars* but also a bit of a *tactile* feel to the haiku!


Moving on to the next example:

> cyclone warning
> by the stove
> I stir my tea

This is a simple *here/there*, but the rainy weather, impending storm, perhaps an old-timey radio and the sound of the flaming stove make this a wonderful *mood piece!*

Note this, especially this particular haiku is not just about the words written on paper, it is the entire ambience that it takes the reader into!


Some of you may think I am overselling it but, trust me, I have *Aphantasia* (you can check out a few *YouTube* videos to know for yourself what that means) but most of my readers, who have normal visualisation skills, have gone gaga over this particular haiku!

Way more than I am physically capable of 😊

In fact, at a recent workshop, this was the haiku that finally brought a photographer around to the haiku mindset, and lit up a smile on his face!

But that neatly brings me to this lovely piece that I am more than capable of swooning over! I have yet to meet a soul, haiku snob or newb, that hasn't loved this one by **Sonali**, and recently talking to a reader smitten by the following haiku I said, and I quote, "Bashō and company can kiss her ass!"

> half moon
> in my window
> half in yours
> — **Sonali Rasal, @SonaliRasalPoetry**

This is such an exceptional visual, firstly!

And so simply done, it's unbelievable! The unbearable, indescribable, ineffable distance and longing between lovers both captured and resolved in such an astoundingly common ubiquitous image – the tired, hackneyed, over-used moon, yet omnipresent and soothing to lovers all the same, since forever!

I doubt there can be a better use of the *here/there* technique either for the depth of the subject or for the brilliance and eloquence of the image – perfectly chosen, and deceptively simply connected!

Hats off, truly!
Continuing my quote from the previous conversation with that reader, "This one by Sonali is my ultimate favourite romantic haiku of all time."

## *Tum nahi samjhogi, Anjali*

On that note, let us talk a bit about this whole business of romance, in the sense of romanticising, in haiku and poetry.

There is no issue with love, emotion, or romantic subjects; one can and must tackle these in haiku, given that all this is quintessential to human existence and *the human experience*, which is the content of haiku.

But there is this not-even-such-a-fine-line-really between *being romantic* on the one hand, and *romanticising* about subjects and scenarios on the other, that a vast majority of writers fail to understand!


And the thing is, in poetry anything goes, in fact the more *romanticised,* and *saccharine,* the image the more the reader is titillated, figuratively speaking. In haiku the price is more on *naturalness,* even erring on the side of *stoicism.*

While there is no problem being poetic in *style* or flowery in *language,* or imaginative in the *imagery,* when the *setup* starts becoming fantastical it somehow doesn't sit right. The connection with truth, and the authenticity of our feeling for the subject somehow becomes suspect, lost in the drama and the glare. It becomes less about the thing you are talking of and more about showmanship, or worse, unreal.

Note this not-so-subtle distinction; especially as poets it is very easy to go down this rabbit-hole of conjuring impossible scenarios, personifying inanimate things and, in general, being overly mushy, grandiose, and dramatic.

But in haiku, we want to know more about *this world*, the here and now, and our connection to it. Remember, as discussed briefly earlier in the piece about the fly, in haiku the goal is to keep the scene as natural as possible.

A bit of talking to, or rather *talking at*, the subjects is fine; praising and comparing to totally unrelated things is okay too, in fact that is required, but not in the way one typically does in poetry which is by making normal objects or animals talk or do totally unnatural things in fantastical scenarios.

Always keep in mind what we are trying to achieve – *we are trying to convey a sudden feeling, or image, we had in a moment, and we are trying to bring the reader to that moment.*

If the fantastical imagery aids with it, and qualifies the object or subject you are talking about, more power to you, but don't try to dazzle the reader with a grand illusion; often easy does it.

The reader, when he reaches that place you so wanted him to inhabit, must not feel it was only smoke and mirrors! Whether you to take him to the clouds or to the ruins of your past, he must believe that once a real person lived here, felt what he feels now...

Why else would he smile or cry for you?

# Ex. #3.5 More examples – now/then

Now, an example of *now/then*:

> even now
> my hands too small –
> Grandma's mittens

One is always small, thinking of dear old *Nanna*, but see how the visual works.

The mittens, of course, would have been big for grandma too, even then; and perhaps now your hands are bigger than what hers ever were, but that's not the point, and you know that!

However, speaking technically now, one immediately *gets* the visual of hands being much smaller than mittens.
But with the eventual reveal of the mittens belonging to grandma, and the clever use of the simple phrases *too small* and *even now*, one quickly understands that the author is talking of his childhood…
And the hands become tinier in your mind!

That, and the fact of mittens being used around the oven might also conjure up the smells of fresh baking, that your mom or grandma did, and the reader is pulled back to his own childhood – the mitts becoming the catalyst to time travel!

Note how visuals and smells generate emotions, and how emotions quickly affect, and often bypass, logical thinking!

Which is why juxtaposition of the right images, with a bit of clever phrasing, can have this huge impact that it does in haiku.

As you can imagine about this *now/then* technique, this *temporal focus shift* might be the most difficult skill to pull off, compared to *here/there* and *big/small*, because it requires you to connect two different times, and perhaps places, through a common theme; typically using a common emotion, or more handy, a common object.

So, here's another example, from a Master:

> this Summer grass
> – the aftermath
> of warriors' dreams
> **– Bashō**

original Japanese text:

> *natsukusa ya*
> *tsuwamonodomo ga*
> *yume no ato*

Bashō expertly spans aeons just looking at a field of overgrown grass that some lords fought and died over centuries ago, only to mix with the dust, eventually – human dreams becoming fodder for common grasslands!

In one fell swoop, the Master putting the might of man and Nature in perspective.

# Ex. #4 Move from line/image to image, and tie it all together

I know this gets very heavy, and difficult, because we are verbal people and are trying to express ourselves through visuals, perhaps for the first time in our lives.

And while we have been trying to get into the mode of visual thinking, we still had to deal with setups and comparisons and eventually use a lot of words, causing a bit of a tug-of-war between our brain's visual and linguistic centres!
So, let's forget these serious exercises for a while and play a game.

I want you to come up with just 2 words (or short phrases), each word being an image, and let them be anything, in fact the farther apart from each other the better. Don't bother about the meaning etc., just come up with 2 totally random visual images, preferably 1-2 words each.

And here's the creative part; now try to link them in the 3rd line, with another image!

So, they can be totally random things, but taken together they somehow must make sense; so, for example,

*wood, strings, guitar!*

Here are some fun examples from my haiku sessions with students:

pickle
grandmother
stories
**- Sonali Rasal, @SonaliRasalPoetry**

That's lovely, and fairly self-explanatory.


Here's another, more convoluted specimen:

parched earth
boop
lick!

In case you didn't get that, the closeup of a dog's nose, especially when dry, looks like really baked *dryland* that's all broken up into polygonal patches 😊


Or how about this; this made people (and myself!) realise that I had got a hang of the essence of haiku:

white car
dyed hair
the politician


One more:

light drizzle
a thousand shivers
Touch-me-not

As you can see, now this is getting more haiku-like as opposed to the barebones *gameplay* of previous examples!

The visual above is, of course, of the shy leaves of the *Touch-me-not* plant folding up in the slightest drizzle, but with a *double entendre* on a romantic *tryst* between lovers!

And finally:

> an old man
> a tiny backpack
> a tiny kid

Again, on the face of it, can be taken as 3 separate visuals, but when the image comes together you may see a loving grandfather carrying his grandkid's schoolbag, himself looking like the small kid following him, and in the process bringing life a full circle.

See, much can be said without saying anything at all, even while having fun and games.

# Ex. #5 Hyperbole

This is another fun exercise, and hopefully poets proper will have most fun this time 😊

*Hyperbole* is an essential part of poetry and even our casual talks for that matter; we all enjoy a bit of grandiosity and fibbing and puffery! We like painting ourselves and our loved ones and heroes in a favourable light.

This exercise is largely about that kind of exaggerating, and what better haiku to introduce it than this lovely masterpiece by the one and only, Kobayashi **Issa**:

> this big the Peony
> says the child
> stretching arms
> **- Issa**

What a sweet image, both of the innocence of childhood and of his delight at the big Peony!
Original Japanese text:

> *kore hodo to*
> *botan no shikata*
> *suru ko kana*

Note however, despite the overselling, that it is still a *natural* image and it still works visually! And it is the visual, of *the child stretching arms*, that actually sells it.


Now, a bit of *standard* exaggerating, for a change:

> panting dog
> — a vacuum
> in the room

This is beyond the realm of possibility, but of course it is obviously understood as so, and yet everyone who's been around a dog can immediately visualise this impossible scenario.
And that's part of the fun in this imagery.

But including this here as more of an exception to the rule. Also note that it simply exaggerates and does not enter the realms of unnecessary fantasizing with soppy tales or anthropomorphised anecdotes.

> ripples in the pool
> the cat
> quite thirsty

Believe it or not, while this works as hyperbole, it is actually a true image, seen with my own eyes! But notice how we use the grandiosity of the visual to accent something else, here the cat's immense thirst!

And that is kind of the point of this exercise, not just over-exaggerating in a vacuum!

Coming to more illustrative examples now:

> busy week –
> the garden slug
> morbidly obese

So, you say you were busy! Note how the writer (yours truly, *as always, when no author mentioned*) expresses his lack of time.
Apparently, he was so busy, and hence unable to tend to his garden, that the *caterpillars* have lived a full life,

feasting on his plants, and are about to *turn in* (hopefully into pretty butterflies)!

But notice, despite the example, the subject of the haiku is not the hyperbolically obese *slug*, that *too* has been *busy* eating, but rather it is the unnoticed passage of time, *suggested by the slug's having chomped so much*, due to the writer's busy work-life!

Again, see the visual storytelling and the intentional use of the phrase *morbidly obese.* Apart from showing the *time-lapse*, it adds a dash of dark humour, given the problems of weight management we all fear, and face, in our *hyperbolically* comically busy lives!
Notice then also the contrast that despite the fairy-tale like narrative and quirky imagery (lifted from *Alice's Adventures in Wonderland*), the picture is still very real, and relevant to our times.


Another, softer issue, and subtler exaggeration:

> lovers' tiff
> even the tide
> sneaks in

A sweet way of putting things; one can indeed infer *Animism* or even *personification* with the Sea quietly trying to overhear gossipy tidings, like the rest of us mortals 😃
However, on closer reading, this is just a clever turn of phrase and the basic visual can still be seen as just a quarrelling couple walking on the beach, with the waves occasionally landing by their feet, as they walk along into the sunset.

# Why so serious?!

Why I stress on *naturalness* this often is because we, especially poets, have a tendency to conjure up fantastical images, comparisons and scenarios, and as harped on many times before, that feels out of place in haiku.

In haiku, the point is to talk through visual metaphors, but while trying to make sure that the visual also works *naturally!* Your scene affects the reader more *viscerally* if he believes he could have walked there some day and felt it by himself...
Because he then wonders how many such moments have passed him by, unknown, unseen...

That is not to say that fantastical or imaginative scenarios are to be avoided, in fact, as we have seen in many examples, that is one of the charms of haiku, to provide and indulge in that kind of childish innocence. Here's one more:

> rifling through
> all the shelves
> Inspector Moth

So, speaking about this example, of course it is a fun fantasy to imagine; but the way a *real* moth goes about banging through your kitchen shelves (though not knocking anything over, poor little soul), it is not far off from reality, just a spicing up of it!

The skill then, is to *ground that image, despite the flights of fancy,* so the reader believes he too could have seen, or imagined, it someday, if he had only walked out and paid attention, outside his busy life and stuck routine and mobile screen; somewhere something real…

That is where the core of haiku lies, at least how I understand it – the imagery suggested or the interpretation can be fantastical, but the basic visual *observed and depicted,* that leads to that *leap* in imagery, should hold true in *real life!*

I feel most beginners, and even some seasoned haiku writers, totally miss this.
Let the reader soar in whatever imaginary skies, but ultimately the tug of the kite string on his hands should cut him true, a feeling he could taste…
By, and for, himself.


All things considered then, try keeping it natural most of the time. But of course, never say never, that is the fun thing about art, anything may work!

And hey, it's *hai-ku,* we are out to play and this exercise is the most license you will ever have of going bananas and trying to make wild things stick!


And of course, you may be a believer in more *romantic* imagery or even *Animism,* so if that's your style go for it!
Don't let my tastes stop you 😊

So, see, whatever works.

While on that topic, don't forget your other figures of speech too!

Just like regular poetry, many of them like *alliteration*, *repetition*, *tautology*, *transferred epithet*, *apostrophe* (especially talking *at*, rather than *to*, something), *euphemism*, *epigram* etc. can work in haiku.

And of course, *metaphor*, *synecdoche* and *metonymy* are the lifeblood of this kind of thinking, as we have seen.


Avoid *similes* though, even in regular poetry *metaphor* is more sophisticated; and especially in haiku *simile* just feels off, of course because a *simile* just tells you out and out that a thing is like another thing.

In a metaphor however, the similarity and recognition unfold in the reader's mind!
This, as we have seen, is the whole fun of haiku, not just for the writer, but also for the reader, this collaborative unravelling of truth!

# Ex. #6 Praise/talk about a thing indirectly

And all of this finally brings us to the point of haiku, at least as I see it. If you have practised all the exercises, and especially if you've used hyperbole well enough to talk about your subject indirectly in the previous exercise, this should be a cake walk.

If not, it is very difficult to write like this, given that we just want to blurt things out at first go.

Not just haiku but much of Japanese culture, or indeed any formal culture, is about diplomacy and subtlety, not saying things out loud.
And art, good art, as they say is all about show, don't tell.


Let's see if we can do that.
We start out very simple:

> Tabebuia –
> even the ravens
> look pretty

No offence to anyone who likes *crows* and *ravens*, and I know a few (some of my best friends like crows 😆) but generally they are not considered beautiful.

This haiku plays on that notion and, using a bit of hyperbole as per the last exercise, brings the spotlight on the beautifully soft pink *Tabebuia* flowers instead, without directly telling the reader how beautiful they themselves are, or even about the effect they have on the writer.

If you've never seen a row of Tabebuia or *Jacaranda* trees in full bloom, by the way, you are missing out a lot in life!

This is one of the trees that got me into haiku, and along with moths (and chicken) remains my favourite haiku motif, even after all these years.
As I like to say, the Japanese can have their Cherry blossoms, we have Tabebuia!

In fact, let's have one more:

> Tabebuia
> to Tabebuia
> I count my years

What more can I, or anyone, praise its beauty – it is my entire *raison d'être!*

These flowers bloom around New Year's, BTW, the *physical natural* (unromantic 😐) reason for the 3rd line, though it was absolutely not necessary here; however, it lets you appreciate the writer's thinking more, when you do know!


Here's another beautiful flower:

> clicking Zinnias
> the pink
> in my cheeks

but speaking of its beauty not with exclamations and adjectives and but by showing the smile of the photographer 😊

Shifting focus from the pink flower to the watcher.

On to other examples, not praising anything now but rather just saying things indirectly:

strong winds
the young crow
lopsided

Of course, the visual is clear and obvious, even a little funny if you are affected by the poor young crow's clumsiness.

But beyond the image, notice the *metaphor*, and I hope this makes you see and reflect about life, and perhaps your own trials and struggles, suggested by the phrase *strong winds*, that made you the experienced person you are today.

the dogs busy
building sandcastles
– winter chill

Walking home in the evenings, you may have seen dogs getting ready for sleep by scuffing up construction sand; this puts the hard life of these strays in a romantic, even childish light, using *euphemism* to soften the blow.

Notice BTW in each of the above examples we are being indirect, but in many technically different ways.

Here's a couple more, more inexplicit examples:

still tangy
at their cores –
old plums

Now, this can just be taken at face value to be about *plums*, and it would still be an okay piece, conveying a decent visual and perhaps even something for the reader's tastebuds.

But when you pay a bit more attention you may observe the use of the words *still tangy* and their contradiction with *old,* and feel that the *epigram*-like structure may be hiding something more.

So, when you take it all together again with *at their cores*, you may think of some very naughty grandpas, or you may take it to mean that despite life's difficulties and reaching an over-ripe middle-age, some folks, perhaps your jovial uncles, may still have maintained a cheerful and fun outlook!


But which is it, or are we reading too much into it?
The answer to all of those is yes!

While some artists, and audiences, like such ambiguity, even for the heck of it, personally I don't!

Still, I would say, as a writer it's up to you, and it's a matter of finding the personal balance that works for your style. Drop as many or as few hints as you wish, but try to make sure the correct interpretation reaches readers – just stop well short of actually telling them though 😃


In any case, the previous example was mostly meant for fun, and to let readers run wild if they take the incomplete hint; not so this next one:

the lilies
bruised pink –
hard rains

While not written specifically for it, this haiku of mine was one of the few chosen by *The Haiku Foundation* for an article honouring the amazing painting by **Frida Kahlo** titled

*Tree of Hope, Remain Strong*
*(Árbol de la esperanza, mantente firme)*

I don't know if you got it, but this is at once more subtle and more clear than the previous ones – a paradox by itself!
It's left entirely to the maturity of the reader, their sensitivity and observation.
There are hinting words, of course – *bruised* and *hard*.

On the face of it, this is just a picturesque scene of *rain lilies* blooming after, well, rains, and the casual reader may leave it there and move on.

However, a more keen, sympathetic reader will find the use of the words *bruised* and *hard* incredibly odd in this sweet picture.

It is this juxtaposition caused by those odd word choices against a beautiful, even peaceful scene, acting as the *Kireji* that can lead you to the other perspective –
is the writer talking of domestic abuse?

Masochism?

Or perhaps the writer just wants us to know that life batters us all, and art and beauty only flower after unbearable suffering.

As mentioned before, the exact content of the trauma or grief is not important, what matters is we both grieve! That one human's mental upheavals reach another, across the page, across time.

Even wordlessly...

# Digestif

Summer walks –
a rain lily
at my dog's spot

# Backbenchers – Work *is* Progress

And just like that we have reached the end of the book.

I hope it was a good class, but like any actual class we will have backbenchers who have not got anything, and those who have understood but need the teacher to show them one more example, though we are done with the whole syllabus.

So here is an example of work in progress:

> even through
> *YouTube* compression
> the river

This is the final version, the thought occurred as I was watching a *YouTube* video titled *Bear sits next to guy*, you may have already watched it.
I had seen versions of this video earlier but was mostly focused on the *bear*, this time around, perhaps because I was part asleep, perhaps because it was better video quality, I actually *heard* the *river*, next to which the *guy* and the *bear* were sitting, and boy, was it something!

You may have noticed though, that the actual haiku does not mention the *bear* at all!

And note this, often you will come up with the idea for a haiku while actually experiencing some event or emotion, in a flash as it were, so later when you try to pen it down, you may try to recapture all the little details of that scene.

But this is a trap!

Remember we are not trying to make a documentary but rather to faithfully capture an emotion or a moment; and in trying to get to the gist of it, as we have learnt in our Exercises, you have to let go of the extraneous.

And sometimes even a big bad *bear* is just a distraction! Remember, the moment was about the deafening impact of the *river*, not the *bear* or the *man* interacting with it.

So, this particular haiku started out as:

> white noise
> a river cuts through
> my thoughts

Now ordinary mortals would be happy calling this a haiku and moving on with their lives; but you and I, dear reader, know the problem with this piece – it talks too much!
It's a decent phrase *cutting through someone's thoughts* and an ok visual of *a river cutting through*, but it's still working more on a verbal level.

And hence I moved on to this:

> white noise
> even through *YouTube*
> the river

Notice here again, I'm still obsessed with *White noise* because I was trying to capture the ironic juxtaposition of people watching *YouTube* videos or using nature sounds to fall asleep and the brutal might of the *river* (or even of *binge-watching*) totally defeating that purpose!

And, just like with the *bear,* I realised even this juxtaposition defeats the purpose of what I am trying to capture here, which is the ruthless power of nature, exemplified here by the *river,* and so I decided to focus on that:

> even through
> *YouTube* compression
> raging river

the happenstance stumbling upon *YouTube* still helping our purpose, diverting the thought in the desired direction.

BTW, if you're not *tech-savvy,* *YouTube* or any digital media will *compress* both the video and audio quality of the actual phenomenon you are capturing on your phone/mic/camera and so, what ultimately reaches the audience is effectively not that *pure* of a *signal.*

But note how we embrace that accidental tangential thought of *YouTube* fully in our haiku and go all *meta* with the idea of *compression* to suggest that we are never *fully experiencing* anything! With that inability, we show the compromises of our modern life away from nature, where we need to experience even a river *thirdhand* on a corporate app!

And we manage a backhanded compliment to nature still, that it can yet reach us, and overpower us, even through this tiny window we have to the world at large that is our mobile phone!

And while I was fairly happy at this point, notice how this is still not the final version!
Though it makes the point, and indeed many more points as explained above, and you could have stopped here, I remember haiku is about subtlety, and this loudness is not my style too.

So instead, we underplay our description, cut out the *raging* adjectives, and let the *river* speak for itself:

> even through
> YouTube compression
> the river

And I hope, as the writer, that the *river* leaves you, the reader, just as speechless!


But of course, we don't just hope, notice how we point the reader carefully not just with the unexpected theory detour of *YouTube compression* but with the thoughtfully placed lowly word – *even!*
As explained above, implying that nature can reach us loud and clear *even* through this noise of the modern world, the river cutting through not just literal mountains but *even* this bad audio quality! ☺


We go for grand gestures, so it is easy to miss this subtlety; it is often the little words that will convey subtle emotion and shift perspective – the *Kireji!*

# Rhythm and Blues

While we have learnt a lot so far, there still remains the thorny issue of rhythm in poetry.

It is difficult to argue that the democratisation of poetry with the advent of *free verse* has been a bad thing, but it also remains a fact that most people who think of themselves as poets have no sense of rhythm!

And in truth, there can be no poetry without rhythm!

Spoken language has its own natural cadence so it has worked out in most cases for conversational poets at *stand-up mics*, but while people understand the importance, even omnipresence, of rhythm in music or dance, they are largely oblivious to rhythm in the written word.

I did not broach this subject till now, as indeed we had other things to understand to be able to write anything worth calling haiku in the first place.
And so, I only occasionally reminded you, trusting the natural rhythm of language and emotion to carry you so far, in most cases.

And while it may be late for many of you to learn about rhythm at this stage in life – indeed there is something to be said about *having an ear* - perhaps it's not too late, or perhaps you are still young and hopeful.

So here comes a standard lesson on rhythm; we learnt this way back, long before the days of the internet, way before people took *free verse* to mean *free for all.*

Rhythm in poetry, or song, or religious epics for that matter, is defined by the *metre* of a *verse*, which can be described as a sequence of *feet*, each *foot* itself being a specific sequence of syllables.

What makes these syllable groups different from each other is which syllables in them are relatively *stressed/unstressed* or *long/short;* you may now remember some of our discussions from earlier about Japanese vs English haiku.

Perhaps the most common *foot* in English literature, and speech, is an *iamb*, which is just one *short/unstressed* syllable followed by a *long/stressed* syllable. It can be heard as the rhythm pattern:

     da-DUM

and some examples of *iambic* words may be:

     a-BOVE, at-TEMPT etc.

*Iambic pentameter*, a common *metre* in English poetry as you'll find e.g., in much of **Shakespeare**, is a sequence of five *iambs;* so, the rhythm of the verse goes:

     da-DUM | da-DUM | da-DUM | da-DUM | da-DUM

Similarly, there are other *feet* e.g., *trochee* which is kinda an *iamb* in reverse, so a *long/stressed* syllable followed by a *short/unstressed* one; some examples:

     DOU-ble, PUMP-kin etc.

Again no one said a *foot* can have only 2 syllables, so you have the *dactyl*, which is *1 long/stressed* syllable followed by *2 short/unstressed* ones e.g., this line by **Robert Browning**:

JUST for a HANDful of SILver he LEFT us …

And we can have other types of *feet* with say, *2 short/unstressed* and *1 long/stressed* syllable (*anapest*), or *both short/unstressed* syllables (*dibrach*), or *both long/stressed* syllables (*spondee*), and so on.

Of course, that's the general pattern, and no one strictly writes each word like that or every poem and song would sound like a band of soldiers marching, but also why e.g., liturgical *shloka* do sound like that!

But the point to note is that the way the syllables stress at certain intervals can greatly affect the mood of the reader, unknowingly.
It is not just the meaning of the words but their *cadence* that unconsciously affects the reader – the internal motion of the ebb and flow of the words' intricacies, the dance of the syllabic *feet*, creates emotion!

While this is lost on most modern amateur poets, and readers, the skilled writer knows this and uses the correct *metre* nonetheless, with clever changes to the *tempo* where needed to betray, or heighten, the reader's expectations and shift the feelings appropriately, either for shock or for little surprises.

How this concerns us in haiku then, is instead of thinking of the **3** *lines* as sections of **5**, **7** and **5** *syllables*, it makes much more sense to *hear* them as a *tetrameter* (4 *feet*) or, thinking musically, as a *bar* of 4 *beats*, or 8 *half-beats*, which indeed is the universal standard in music!

So, taking our model length example by Bashō again:

*furuike ya*
*kawazu tobikomu*
*mizu no oto*

| 1 | 2 | 3 | 4 | 5 | 6 | 7 | 8 |
|---|---|---|---|---|---|---|---|
| fu | ru | - | i | ke | ya | - | - |
| ka | wa | zu | - | to | bi | ko | mu |
| mi | zu | no | - | o | to | - | - |

it is easy to see that this is a lyrical, even musical, piece of 8 *half-beats* with 3, 1 and 3 *half-beat pauses* left in the lines for effect (or breathing space).

This is a much more logical and, given how we sing, and even just speak, natural way to look at it rather than at the *occupied* 5, 7 and 5 *syllables!*

This also neatly explains why sometimes more or less syllables work in some haiku.
Because just as in song, even if the lyric ends early, or occasionally if you cram more words in, you keep the beat going, regardless!

And in haiku of 2 lines, it is a *pentameter* again of 10 *half-beats*, with 1 or 2 *half-beat pauses* only, per line,

thus giving us the **8/9** or **9/8** patterned haiku of, again –
and count it – **17** *syllables!*

Or even just the regular **4**-*beat* verse in **2** lines with
only **1** skipped *half-beat* per line, giving us the **7/7**
syllable verses that were standard in *Renga* (and of
which the *Hokku* used to be the opening verse)!

See, how neatly it all fits.


And just as with the different kinds of poetic *feet*
mentioned earlier, the pauses we take and the syllables
we stress, especially along with the *hardness* or
*softness* of certain sounds, will inform the reader of the,
often hidden, *subtext* of the haiku.

The subtly hinted mood behind the carefully chosen
word sounds churning the sensitive reader's emotions
within the writer's cleverly orchestrated flow!

And the pauses don't just qualify the words, the subtle
stresses indeed imbue them with more meaning than
the writer wants to let on, and that the *tone-deaf* reader
is indeed capable of comprehending!

What is left unsaid, the blanks, are often more
important than the words expressed; this is certainly
true in haiku, and it turns out, in more ways than one!


And that, good folks, is how to haiku!

# Parting shots, some for the road

A few words before we part; the way the exercises are structured, with so many formalities and proprieties, you may feel a bit stressed that certain things must always be done so; but that's not true in haiku, art, or life – the fact is that anything may work.

The various exercises and tips mentioned in the book are just guidelines to get your creative juices flowing and to provide a robust channel to direct your wild untamed ideas.
However, nothing is set in stone, use this structure to jump off of, and develop your own thoughts and style.

Of course, it is our job as a haiku writer to write, and direct, effectively but, especially as a beginner, things can be tough; not only are you trying to express visually, which may be a new and difficult thing by itself, but you are also trying to say things indirectly, which can be really tough.
So, an easy hack is to *bring the writer into the scene* and *talk to, or at, objects*. That allows you to speak your mind without disturbing the sanctity of the *natural* scene, and given that most haiku springs up suddenly as a reflection in a moment, it is fair that the writer be talking out aloud.

Having been given this license though, use it sparingly for it can become all tell and no show, and can become soppy really quickly, and also be limiting to your creativity as an artist. Use it as a crutch only when you see no other way to express, and better yet, as you

grow and become more adept at writing, use it only when it adds to the effect or to the moment.
So, some examples to get you started:

> against the storm
> the spider's web –
> I hold my breath

Here, bringing in the author not only makes this a personal *Nat Geo* styled narration, but seeing the cleverly hidden hyperbole that the author does not want to breathe so as not to get the spider in more trouble makes this a very visceral experience for the reader, and elevates it above the documentary status!
It also lets us know about the author, that he cares about the underdog despite being a helpless bystander, just like the *Nat Geo* cameraman, to the whims of nature.


Or when Issa says this

> You must see Matsushima
> I apologise little fleas
> I can't let you go
> **- Issa**

to the fleas he's carrying in his luggage and indeed on his body, it tells us not only of his love for all life, even bloodsucking insects, but it *apotheosizes* the beauty of the *Matsushima* islands to the level of *Teertha Kshetras* – that he cannot let even fleas miss their beauty!

Beauty as salvation, who would have thought 😊
And hundreds of haiku have been written, before and after, glorifying *Matsushima*, but then there is only the one Issa.

What this technique, of the *writer talking at the object*, can also do, as we've seen in some examples before, is add a childlike innocence to the author, and reader, and a fairy-tale like quality to the scene:

> what dress
> should I wear
> Moth in closet

This bypasses the reader's reservations altogether, allowing them to indulge in these childish charades. As mentioned before, such innocence and child-like perspective are highly prized in haiku, and this can be a quick and dirty way to catch the reader off-guard.


Another quick hack is to just paint a picture without really bothering about any deep meaning or even any techniques or anything. Sometimes, if the image itself is powerful, that can be enough:

> storm clouds —
> a snail
> in *hyperlapse*

A picture says way more than a thousand words, and that is sometimes enough to floor the reader!
Here's another simplistic piece:

> a villa
> with a Bouganvilla —
> a Bouganvilla!

relying simply on the reader's love of the flower, expecting them to have been amazed some day in their life having seen the bright deep pink flowers in someone's bungalow!

Relying on it so much in fact that even a pun has been attempted with suspect spelling!

But keep in mind, as mentioned before, these are just hints to get you writing; what will actually help you write is your own life experiences, the things you know, the scenes you are familiar with, what you see daily around and within yourself.

You may want to talk of beauty and great vistas and mountains and skies, but if all you have around you is gutters and stray dogs and concrete cages, work with that!

I told you earlier that one of my most common haiku motifs is *chicken*, turns out I wasn't kidding:

> roomier
> by evening
> the chicken cage

or

> still warm
> in my carry bag
> the chicken

Sometimes no ornamentation is needed, just a well-placed observation can pierce the heart!

After all haiku isn't just about rainbows and unicorns and child-like *innocence*, a studied *world-weariness* and *detachment* are equally common and highly appreciated subjects in haiku, and especially in *Senryu*.

But either way, don't let your lack of experience or knowledge become a limiting factor.

They say in Chinese (it's not actually a Chinese saying, that was just a made-up story) there's a curse *to live in interesting times* – and that may still be true, especially in our current political, economic, and real physical climate!

But even if you wish to live a shielded life, at least read good books, and watch documentaries; gain knowledge, surf the world wide web and cast a wide, wide net!

And don't limit yourself to just poetry or haiku or even music; learn about engineering, and sports or economics, or stamp collecting, or sheep shearing, whatever floats your boat – even carpentry, on that note!

The wider the field of view of your passions, the more similarities you'll see in everyone and everything, and there will be infinitely more material and opportunities, not just for haiku, but for an overall fulfilled life!

Read, read a lot – no knowledge is ever wasted!

Coming back to more practical tips, all this visual jugglery may be too much for us not just in the beginning but to find consistently, even down the line; it helps to remember then that though a visual art, haiku is ultimately written!

And so, being merchants of words, sometimes we can pull off verbal tricks to make up for the lack of imagery:

> thro' the cobbles
> a shoe flower

this *pun* on *cobbles* implying the stones and suggesting the visual of *cobblers* by the streets, and then deflecting to the *Hibiscus*, or *Shoe flower*, through the connecting word *shoe!*

Or this wonderful piece by **Mahrukh**:

> cornfield carpet –
> soft and silent
> an earful too
> **- Mahrukh N Bharucha**

evoking not just images but even sound through a brilliant *pun* with the clever use of the word *earful.* In case you didn't get it, they are called *ears* of corn!

Pay attention to the words, it is often the little words that will hint at the mood and subtly shift the reader's focus to alternative perspectives; we have discussed this at length in talking of the *Kireji.*

However, even generally, one more example:

> snatched flowers
> on a plate –
> pooja day
> **- Manjusha, @Purse_pictive**

Some of you may miss the subtle irony created here by **Manjusha**, by the careful choice of the word *snatched*, saying much about our relation to God and Nature, and the *nature* of our *spirituality*, while trying not to be disrespectful to believers.

Coming to more technical linguistic stuff, pay attention also to the *line order*.

This is not even about haiku really; any good story or even joke requires a proper *setup*, *build-up* and *delivery*, or *punchline*, that creates and releases the tension or humour, as the case may be.

> city streets
> way past bedtime
> a cricket chirps

So compared to the one that will follow, this line order maintains the suspense better – till the very last line you are thinking of *city folks*, of the urban author or yourself perhaps.
And then the sudden appearance of the *Cricket* instead may make you smile at the surprise or sad that the circadian rhythm of even insects suffers thanks to human enterprise.

On the other hand,

> city streets
> a cricket chirps
> way past bedtime

perhaps some may find this rhythm better.

This may make you feel more lonely, especially when you see the *Cricket* as a *metaphor* for someone roaming alone in the city, late into the nights.

And though this lets go of the suspense altogether, unlike the first version, there is something to be said about delivering a sad line simply, without any ornamentation, as we have noted earlier too.

And while we are talking about lines, you may find it helps you to write in 2 lines rather than 3 – that feels much more natural, and more importantly, easier, in English.
Don't fight it, go with the flow, it's a different language, with many other restrictions too, so why make it more difficult than it has to be; for example:

> off with one shoe
> Cinderella pup

Where exactly would one fit a 3rd line in that?
Any break would feel unnatural:

> off
> with one shoe
> Cinderella pup

or unnecessarily gaudy, though it may be acceptable nowadays in a modern expressive style of writing.

Even in haiku of 3 lines, it often helps in English to have a longer 1st line, normal 2nd line and a very short 3rd line, often just one word, as opposed to the *short-normal-short*, 5-7-5, pattern in Japanese:

This is because in English, the setup often needs to be done in the 1st line, and that takes words, lots of them!

Of course, like everything else, this depends on a case-to-case basis and there are plenty of haiku, even in this book, following the normal pattern.
However, it's good to know you have options.

Don't get stuck in the *is this how the Japanese do it?* mindset; for the last time, this is not Japanese, we are writing haiku in English!
Know and notice the nuances, and limitations, of your language, and indeed in your own self, and work with that – after all haiku is all about paying attention!

Speaking of, one thing that you may have read about haiku, but perhaps noticed that we haven't talked about at all, at least not directly, is *juxtaposition* and *contrast*.

These are of course important concepts, and though we didn't have exercises specifically for them, you may remember that we have successfully used these techniques by choosing proper images and shifting focus. Why we didn't fuss over *juxtaposition* and *contrast* separately though, is because you shouldn't actually think and write like that!

They are good techniques but, no matter what anyone told you, not mandatory, as indeed we have seen in the

many examples in this book; and worse, you run the risk of falling into a bad habit of always thinking in black and white!
And of course, life is never that simple, and haiku, being a reflection of life, must flourish in the shades missed in between!

But hey, if you are stuck in a rut then it can be easier to think in dualities, and many examples can be readily available. Here are a few:

> the first leaves of Spring
> — and first snails

A simple observation, yet a powerful one, showing both the blooming and destruction of life in one image!


But of course, not all comparisons need to be this heavy or world-impacting!
Here's one in a much lighter vein:

> the shades
> and the lights —
> white Hibiscus


And then again, as you get better, not all comparisons need to be between objects or even directly obvious:

> new day
> a cat or a chicken
> screams somewhere

A *senryu* indirectly showing the weariness of the author through a comical depiction of the many ways one may have no semblance of peace and quiet in this loud existence – the *contrast* here being the dashing of the *hopes* of a new day *against* the tired *realisation* that all days are equally irritating!

Point to note is that *contrast* and *juxtaposition* are just techniques to easily make connections and disparities visible to the reader.
However, as shown in the exercises, we don't need to be ham-fisted about it, and often just shifting focus will show similarities and differences much more strongly, even in things not necessarily visibly opposed, or linked, to each other, as it is in normal life – the haiku revealing hidden connections and contradictions that are obvious in hindsight!

And as a bonus, it even affords readers the chance to interpret all this for themselves!

For the same reasons, another supposedly important aspect of haiku that we have skipped is the *surprise ending*, shifting focus is a much subtler way of doing that, rather than trying to be clever about it crudely, and the *deflection* is occasionally surprising to the reader, as we seen in many examples earlier.

So, you may have read "haiku" on the internet where the 3rd line comes totally *out of left field*, say:

> Haikus are easy.
> But sometimes they don't make sense.
> Refrigerator.

and while it is a good laugh, sometimes, I hope it is clear to us by now, this is not haiku, and not just because of the ultra-long 2nd line.

In fact, this is not even good writing technique, using a
*Deus ex machina!*
Whenever there is a surprise intended, hints to it must
be cleverly and subtly hidden in the previous lines, that
become apparent on a *double take*.

Why lay readers are shocked when reading haiku with
surprising last lines – and not all haiku use *deflection*,
as we have seen in many examples – is because they
cannot read haiku like we have learnt to, and they miss
the hints entirely.
Or perhaps they have read some of the much prevalent
badly written haiku, as above, only intended for shock
purposes, because the writers themselves have no clue
– a situation that this book hopes to remedy.


We have seen examples of well-placed hints and subtle
*deflection* earlier in the exercise on shifting focus and
other places, but here are some more direct examples
where the purpose is only to achieve that surprise:

> Dad's gift –
> the wrapping full
> of fingerprints

Here again, the *fingerprints* don't come out of the blue,
but rather the first line leaves that ambiguity where you
may expect it to be a gift *from dad* (and he may be
rather clumsy!) but the picture reverses itself and
reveals it to be a gift *to dad* from his little ones!

Or here:

> everyone else
> just green with envy
> Tradescantia

the lovely purple leaves of the *Spiderwort* or *Purple Heart* plant are being hinted at earlier by *everyone else* and *just green.*

And of course, sometimes it can be just fun and no hinting is needed:

> cold nose
> the reassuring warmth
> of WhatsApp

however here too the *WhatsApp* is not out of place; it's just a pun and alternate source of the *warmth* needed in the *cold* lonely lives of modern folks!

But sometimes, apart from the surprise, meant to take you off-guard, it can be very well-crafted still, which is ideally how it should be:

> 1000 paper cranes
> getting better
> with dad's diapers

Presenting the other end of life than that portrayed in the first example here, the *diapers* too don't come out of nowhere, though it's a remarkable leap of imagination from the *origami* in the 1st line!

But the difficulty and skill, both physical and emotional, of getting *tape-style* diapers wrapped correctly around your aging invalid father, year in year out, mirrors perfectly the emotion of the ritual of crafting a 1000 paper cranes with your *life partner* for the wish of a happy life, or for someone's recovery...

Happy as can be, or what recovery life allows 

And now for the last recommendation for budding haiku poets, choose the proper *motifs!*

This can happen by accident, and observation, of course, as much haiku sprouts spontaneously as you get deeply moved by a flower or a sunset or some other event in nature or some happening in your surroundings.
And likely that object will fit correctly your haiku's intended emotional effect.

However, often all you will have is a diffuse emotion, and you will need to work out the proper flower or animal etc. as an illustration, to fit the mood of your piece; some obvious examples being *cats* for *laziness, curiosity* etc.


But to see how vastly different emotions can hit just by changing the central object, kind of what happened earlier with the *rocking chair* (that wasn't even the main motif of that haiku, it was the *crescent*), see these two examples that follow:

> the Peony unfolds
> a hundred layers
> I'd never known

The overall happy mood is perceptible, and the feeling that even something so nonchalantly humble as the common *Peony*, when observed in detail, can be such a source of joy unfolding, in layers, is a delightful sentiment indeed!
And it makes the reader wonder how many simple joys we miss!

And then look at this:

A similar looking but much more menacingly named flower, the *Black Narcissus Dahlia* changes the entire theme of the piece even though it is still the exact same imagery of a big, layered flower unfolding as it blooms, and us being unaware of simple facts!

Here you will think not of happiness, but of some horrible (hopefully ex) relationships; or perhaps even just a cool sly seductress from *Bond* or some *noir* films 

And of course, it wasn't as simple as just changing the central flower; even the rhythm of the two pieces affects the mood in those intentionally different ways, if you caught it!

Pay attention.
This is also where haiku betrays its linguistic roots!

No matter how much *cinephiles* want to appropriate the art, poets not only have *wordplay* at their disposal but also *words,* simple regular words, have *connotations* and *symbolism*, which can so easily be used to cleverly divert readers to alternate perspectives, if the words are chosen well.

So, think about them before, and even after, putting them on paper. Practice these skills, write, and rewrite a lot, and you should get good in due time.

And take time, don't give yourself airs just because you wrote one good haiku, anyone can do that by accident!

To paraphrase Bashō, anyone can bask in reflected lightning for a moment, and still be very much in the dark!

> by lightning
> men are illumined
> even in this world
> **- Bashō**

Original Japanese text:

> *inazuma ni*
> *satorenu hito no*
> *tōtosa yo*

He is of course referring to, and like us immediately discarding, the concept of *satori*, sudden enlightenment, that is still so hip in our days!

So, just to let you know, all the English haiku given as examples above in this book, other than those that are mine, are by my students. And reading those you may believe they are very good writers of haiku (as indeed some of them are).
However, much of their other work is still quite rudimentary, or in certain cases, non-existent – they simply haven't written much else at all!


The game is consistency.

It is only when you can churn out piece after piece of *acceptable* quality on any topic you felt anything at all about, and *in your personal style*, and readily find images to illustrate any given emotion or concept that you or your friends may be stuck on, that you can learn to relax a bit and accept that you may have finally arrived!

Take that in, when you do, because you will never see the world with old eyes, ever again!
And then, keep writing, and share that view with the world!


And even then, not every haiku you embark on will be smooth sailing, sometimes you will get stuck on a simple stupid 2/3-liner piece of poetry for a long, long time, and you will see days turn into weeks turn into months, sometimes even years and still you may not be exactly happy with your previous attempt!

That's the sorrow of every artist who wants to do a good job; the ants working, pulling much more than their weight, while the crickets go out and sing!

There's no consolation, as they say, virtue is its own reward...
Play on!


(And by that, I mean slog on!)

# What? How!

Only one last thing to share then, and this is not about *topic* or *technique* but rather *tone*.
As the eminent film critic Roger Ebert loved to say, *"It's not what a movie is about, it's how it is about it."*


That is not to say that your topics and emotions are not important, and of course, it depends both on the subject matter and your own style but, as discussed in the very beginning, it is very easy to become very serious about all this and write as if you were bearing the cross or carrying the whole world on your shoulders!

It helps to remember then, in haiku, and particularly in senryu, it is also seriously important, and indeed effective, not only to shed light on truth (even *Truth*, if there is such a thing) but also to make light of it!


So, taking this example again:

> the lilies
> bruised pink –
> hard rains

this talks of some serious hurts, and some deep and ugly truths, like the blossoming of beauty only through hardship or even abuse, among other interpretations.

And the topic being deathly serious, no wonder the writer (*yours truly*) takes a very serious tone; and no issues with that, and indeed it's a celebrated haiku.

But now read this:

Summer walks –
a rain lily
at my dog's spot


Doesn't this say much the same thing, perhaps even worse things, even using the same *motifs* – *rain lily* and *rain* (or other more doubtful methods of irrigation)!

But it does that through an entirely different perspective and imagery and mood, and see how much that softens the blow!

And what else is humour for if not to help us survive through this – life taking a piss on your existence, quite literally in this one!


Again, it's not just about humour, but how you approach your piece. Mind not just your words, mind your tone.
Pay attention…

And have fun, it's hai–ku!

# Hototogisu

To summarise, we as haiku poets, stand at a unique intersection of words and visuals.

Indeed, *imagery* in poetry is nothing new, it's just not used as much with the kind of poetry people have been churning out over the past few decades under the guise of *free verse*.
In that sense haiku is just a small part of poetry.

But haiku doesn't just pay lip service to imagery, instead it takes the metaphorical baton, or scissors, and runs with it!

Once one gets it into their head that writing haiku involves not just writing with a different frame of mind but indeed requires seeing with an entirely different perspective, that it is a *mode switch*, things become considerably simple and intuitive.
In fact, it becomes impossible not to see haiku in everything around you, in all the little moments; waking up to the sun's soft touch, having a silent bath, your long daily commutes in the bus or sitting under the stars, or just watching the little mutts playing in the alleys.

You will find that inspiration strikes everywhere, and *reflection* can happen anywhere!

But in the beginning, with the wide world of opportunities and techniques now at your feet you may feel an *embarras de richesse* and find yourself paralysed by the infinite choices, not knowing where even to start.

Well, it is customary in haiku to start by writing about the *Cuckoo!*
It is an interesting little bird when you think about it.

You can talk of its sweet voice, or its ugly black looks, including whether black implies ugliness or even about the Capitalist commodification of that anger, if you want to go even more *meta!*

Or the fact that the bird is even so hard to spot!
Or that it is a wicked thing, hijacking other birds' nests!

Or perhaps you may feel sad that it grows up an orphan in a hostile unknown world...

Also, since it is migratory, the Japanese considered the Cuckoo to be a messenger from the heavens!
And they even have a beautifully perfect **5**-*syllable* name for it – not that we care about syllable-counting now after all this, I hope! – *Hototogisu*.

Whatever your angle, write about it. Or not!
Write about anything you want!


And with that, my farewell:

> I keep turning
> to the window –
> Cuckoo

Your move.

# Further reading

inch by inch
year on year
growth rings

*The Classic Tradition of Haiku* by Dover Publications is a must-have for any serious haiku writer or reader.

And while Bashō is ubiquitous and indeed synonymous with haiku to most of us, I would recommend Takarai **Kikaku**, perhaps his best, and wildest, student, and the one with whom I feel most kinship. My favourite:

> "It is my snow!"
> – thinking thus
> my hat lightens
> **- Kikaku**

The original Japanese text

> *waga yuki to*
> *omoeba karushi*
> *kasa no ue*

also has a play on words with the *karu* (from the word *karushi*) in the 2nd line reminding of *Summer* that contrasts with the *snow, yuki,* in the 1st line, while also hinting at the eventual *enlightenment* of his thought!


And then there is this celebration of *Hedonism*, while still under the wings of his ascetic Master, Bashō himself:

> among Morning Glories
> I feast –
> that's the man I am
> **- Kikaku**

The original Japanese text:

> *asagao ni*
> *ware wa meshi kū*
> *otoko kana*

Also, this contemplation on the *Simulation Hypothesis* before it was cool – actually it was cool in Eastern philosophy way before Western audiences watched *The Matrix* and got their brains scrambled!

> bitten by a flea
> in dreams or in truth
> – sleep marks
> **- Kikaku**

The original Japanese text:

> *kiraretaru*
> *yume wa makoto ka*
> *nomi no ato*

Or just this simple existential reflection, proving he was worthy of his Master after all:

> tiny tree frog
> riding a Banana leaf
> how we sway
> **- Kikaku**

The original Japanese text:

> *amagaeru*
> *bashō ni norite*
> *soyogi keri*

BTW, the word *Bashō* means a *Banana* plant!

Bashō took it as his pen name when gifted a, rare for Japan then, *Banana* tree – the more you know 😊

But of course, my Master will always be Kobayashi **Issa**; often derided for his over-sentimentality, even now people miss his visual imagery while dismissing his work as not *proper* haiku!

But who else can write with such simple gut-wrenching power:

> this Rice planter –
> a child bawls
> and her row veers
> - Issa

Even with his detractors, this is considered by many scholars to be the greatest poem in the Japanese language; the original Japanese text:

> *saotome ya*
> *ko no naku hō e*
> *uete yuku*

And despite knowing such great pathos who else can muster such profound empathy and innocence:

> o come let's play
> my parents are away,
> orphan Sparrow
> - Issa

Even more heart-breaking when you know that Issa lost his mother quite early in life, and was treated very badly by his stepmother; the original Japanese text:

> *ware to kite*
> *asobe yo oya no*
> *nai suzume*

Or just this simple recognition, again, of the effect of beauty, and finding human oneness:

> in the shade of flowers
> we are strangers
> no more
> **- Issa**

The original Japanese text:

> *hana no kage*
> *aka no tanin wa*
> *nakari keri*

Or just this wonderful image and deflection:

> the snow thaws
> and the village floods
> with children
> **- Issa**

Issa, as you may have noticed, has a solid grip on childhood, innocence, strong visuals, and above all, wonderful observation, not just emotions.
The original Japanese text:

> *yuki tokete*
> *mura ippai no*
> *kodomo kana*

And so many, many more amazing pieces by Issa!

*Write like Issa: A Haiku How-To* by **David G. Lanoue** is a must-read to understand the intricacies of haiku beyond just the technicalities.

Apart from the wonderful Masters featured here, I particularly enjoy the work of a contemporary haiku poet **Ivan Akhmatov**, who goes by ___ta_to___ on *Instagram*.

You may have to translate many of his pieces, but they are worth it, and even translated, very poetic!
Here's an example, as you won't take my word for it, here's my translation 😛

> through the window
> the night stumbles
> into my teacup
> - ___ta_to___

Here's a couple more, translated by the poet himself:

> On this May night,
> The moon smells of lilac.
> Sing, nightingale! Sing!
> - ___ta_to___

> The house is empty...
> And now you are orphans,
> Apple blossoms.
> - ___ta_to___

**Irina Guliaeva** is a fun artist with haiku published in many online journals and regularly featured in *Mainichi*, the very reputed Japanese newspaper.

And apart from her lovely haiku she also posts amazing pics on *Instagram*, you'll see what I mean, do check her out.

water under the snow
found by chance
mum's diary
**- Irina Guliaeva, @IrinaGuliaeva_lit**

alone
at its
height
white
crayon
**- Irina Guliaeva, @IrinaGuliaeva_lit**

Here also observe the modern technique of typing visually.
You may say it's not-so-modern, as Japanese haiku was always written top to bottom (though in syllables), but this here was done for visual effect, to mirror the height of the crayon 😀

And then there is this killer pun

opening buds
my daughter's first
pepper spray
**- Irina Guliaeva, @IrinaGuliaeva_lit**

while still talking of such a serious topic!
Irina rocks!

Closer home, there's a *Marathi* haiku poet, **Hema Gotkhindikar**, whose book I found totally by providence! Do check out her हायकू तुझे-माझे (Haiku – Yours and Mine) published by Bharari Prakashan.

One of the examples of her soft sorrows:

> the bird has flown
> a green twig
> quivers still
> **- Hema Gotkhindikar**

How beautifully she talks of the passing away of her husband, her loneliness, and fears of the long life she still has ahead of her!
The original Marathi text:

> पक्षी उडाला
>
> डुलतच राहिली
>
> हिरवी फांदी

Here's another lovely *existential* example:

> droplets in puddles
> on leaves, in the flowers
> droplets all
> **- Hema Gotkhindikar**

though the same haiku could also have a happy interpretation!

> lakes refreshed
> leaves, and flowers
> bathed fresh
> **- Hema Gotkhindikar**

The original Marathi text:

तळ्यात थेंब
पानात नि फुलात
थेंबच थेंब

And finally, this amazing combination of astonishingly simple, but colourful, imagery and masterful wordplay:

the Bougainvillea
so full of colour
yet not a scent
- **Hema Gotkhindikar**

This does not translate well because a couple of the Marathi words used have a subtle double meaning, so I have stuck more to the imagery, above.

But the literal translation would be something like:

like a Bougainvillea
so full of life
tho' utterly clueless
- **Hema Gotkhindikar**

The original Marathi text:

बोगनवेल
किती रंगात न्हाते
गंध नसू दे

Do read a lot of *Instagram* accounts, *Facebook* pages and even online journals and published magazines, and books.

A cautionary note here, though; getting published is not a seal of quality!
Foremost, remember our techniques and cross-check with the wide variety of published, and even awarded, haiku even in reputed journals, and you will soon discover much mediocre work, some frankly insulting in its lack of artistic merit!

Various editors have their own opinions, and agendas, or sometimes just some theme for a particular month's issue.
So let that not be your driving force, to be selected, and don't rest on your laurels either, if featured somewhere!


I hope this book has provided you the requisite arsenal; form your own opinions on what are good standards of writing and develop your creativity on your own terms.

And keep writing!

## *Yours truly*

**More books, and collections of my haiku coming soon. Sharing below some of my work published so far.**


**To Live Here**, a haiku anthology by *The Wee Sparrow Poetry Press.*

> another town
> perhaps some day
> – dandelions


**The Cold Moon Journal:**

> a dozen moons –
> slicing onions


**The Haiku Foundation:**

> here I stand
> watch me too
> passing cloud


> limping dog –
> the pigeons shuffle
> just a little


> 1000 paper cranes
> getting better
> with dad's diapers

the lilies
bruised pink –
hard rains

Meantime you can find me on *Instagram* **@lovelifeetc**

Apart from the haiku, if you'd like to support my poetic endeavours, you can find my well-received, though not enough sold 😄 book of poems, **Siamese Compassion**, on Amazon, scan the QR Code:

Another book of poems is in the works.

From that, one of my newer poems *Duryodhan Takes One Below the Belt* was published in the lovely anthology **A Map Called Home**, by Kitaab Singapore.
You can find that on Amazon too:

Or if you like your poems light, there's another book of poems, **A Trans-Arabian Handshake**, on the various manifestations of love, written over a period of 2 decades!

## ABOUT THE AUTHOR

Kaushal Suvarna was born in the East but educated in Western thought and has spent the greater part of his 41 years on earth thinking and experimenting on love, morality, and life in its myriad shades, dabbling in literature, chess, music, movies, cosmogony, quantum mechanics, psychology, neurology, genetics, philosophy, and spirituality, grabbing an MSc in Mathematics along the way before retiring to work in IT.